YIELD SIGNS DON'T EXIST

POEMS BY

KATHRYN IONATA

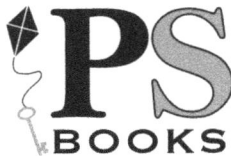

PS BOOKS

Regional Publishing, National Voice
A division of Philadelphia Stories

PS
BOOKS

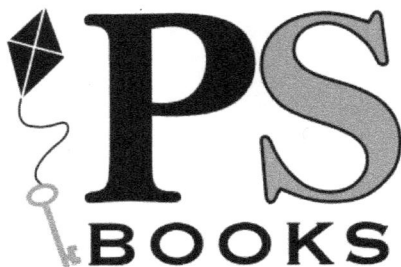

Regional Publishing, National Voice
A division of Philadelphia Stories

PS Books
93 Old York Road
Ste. 1-753
Jenkintown, PA 19046
www.psbookspublishing.org

Published by PS Books,
a division of Philadelphia Stories, Inc.
ISBN

Cover Image: ©2016 Allison R. Mosher
Cover & Book Design: Andrew Whitehead

To Mike

TABLE OF CONTENTS

AFTER THE FIRE

After the fire, we found coins,
edges barely charred.
We found coins, not sliced
black and white memories
of children—now grown and bent
to unearth, they garner only soot
(they will wash their clothes more than once
to be rid of the smoke). No,
the only faces preserved are presidents'.

We found coins, not a Stradivarius
(left by Germans during the war)
or even its wood splintered remains.
Not passports stamped in Naples, 1953,
(to have a job meant to sail
where automobiles
bunched close like sheep).

We didn't find tiny spoons,
black before the fire,
or airmail letters announcing births.
We found coins, not a sewing kit,
cushions bursting spikes. We found coins,
not a vegetable garden, exploded tomato guts and
    timid basil,
not art projects or velvet sofas or knick-knacks.

There was only ash to excavate.
We found a family nickeled and dimed, but
not wooden forks, not a lace dress,
but coins,
only coins.

VEGETARIAN

Reno trapped a turkey
up in some Bucks County woods,
brought it back to Philly in a sack.
He leashed it in the cellar,
next to the eel tank.
Turkey shit over *Inquirer* headlines.

On wobbly legs, Baby Joe climbed
the stairs each day to visit.
He babbled tales of castles,
horses, princes.
Feathers in chubby fists.

You can snap a turkey neck with one hand,
take a cleaver to the head. Dead,
done. Thanksgiving now,
Mom slit the throat to bleed out
over hours. Baby Joe watched
his friend's eyes twitch, glaze.
Cockscomb red stretched across concrete,
carpet unrolled for a tiny king.

CATHOLIC GIRLHOOD

Take hair that ripples like wildfire
    Extinguish it when light
shatters the cloudy skyline,
when skirt length must prove obedience.
At night, imagine greeting your boyfriend
with hair worn like a mermaid.

Spend time behind the red velvet curtain
on bent knees. Whisper through
the screen with a voice full of gravel.
    Deepen when telling sins. Soften when telling
    lies.

Hold the wafer in a hot mouth—never let teeth
break through. Sip bitter wine
from the cup—cleaned, offered, cleaned.
Later, stand huddled in the woods by the rectory
with a decanter from someone's coat.
    Feel your throat burn. Like it.

On the night of the dance, see the crucifix
over your date's shoulder—and forget it
in the backseat of the car, where windows
steam to hide you. Bend knees
as he slides crinolines up your thighs.
    Make the sign of the cross:
a kiss on the lips, chest,
collarbone, earlobe.

And when asked if you pray every night,
say, Yes, Sister, with your face open
like a white lily newly bloomed.

WHEN YOU BECAME A NUMBER

Yesterday I saw a child,
cowboy in training,
fire his first toy gun.
He whipped through
his mother's legs, shot
at trees, dogs, mailboxes,
and I remembered—

only thirty-four days before:
You played barber, perched on the tub
in your phone booth-sized bathroom.
I watched clumps of honey-colored hair
float to the floor like gossamer ghosts.
Now, you said, they got one less head to shave.

I helped you pack your duffel bag:
toothbrush, boxer shorts, *Playboy.*
Your house a still void,
only sirens and shouts
from the next row house over
poked holes through the silence.

You stood over me:
eighteen-and-a-half years, six foot one,
hand-me-down jeans,
brown eyes, vision 20/40,
bruise over left brow from a wild drum solo;
history of seasonal allergies,
all the necessary shots—
private ready to report for duty
in seventeen hundred hours.

Were you once that little boy?
If your mother knew then
what she knows now
would she
have given you
a different toy to play with?

SHE DOESN'T KNOW WHERE SHE IS. SHE KEEPS ASKING ME HOW I GOT HERE.

Hands cold like glaciers, i, i, iss, ice
Voice of words, melting voice, white crystals melt,
each unlike the last, a white blanket on the ground

Ocean eyes, ocean, lake, water, come on in the
      water's great,
eyes look like the breakfast man's, the man from
      breakfast
he knows her gives her hard candies to suck on
holds her hands when they wriggle on their own.
Do I know you?

The young man holds her hand now, he is less cold
      now
she is not afraid of him he is long limbs and pale
      skin
like the little boy living in the picture frame
she would like to see the little boy
but she likes this man too he says it's *snowing* outside

and it will be a *white Christmas.*
White like the ground when she was a girl,
carving angels with her arms, wearing Jack's scarf
letting flakes melt on her tongue,
a snow kiss, he said.

BREAKDOWN

For Tom Cruise

There is no such thing as a breakdown.
Pieces of your mind   fly loose
        like roof shingles
                    in a hurricane
        but when the storm sleeps,
peace will reign again

Words spout from your lips,
mistimed water balloons
        that hit   targets
    with wet shock, a force
you couldn't predict.   You'll learn
        to hold back

People are paper dolls, flat
characters who charm   or hurt
        and you bang them together,
        make friends, make friends.

There is no such thing as a breakdown.
Replace the rattle of a pill bottle
        with good old-fashioned remedies
and feel your world unpuzzle

VIEWING

They said her sunken cheeks were pumped full of
    life,
her white hair pruned full and dense,
when all her life it had been slippery fine.

Her hands were probably folded
across her belly, fingers stripped
of gold bands that have fallen since to daughters.

I would rather remember the woman
who kissed pictures of angels, crafted crosses from
    palms.
She could slice strawberries thin as photographs
with hands scarcely larger than a child's.

When they closed the lid that afternoon in May
it was weighed down with roses, bittersweet pinks
and chirping yellows, and I wished I had asked her
her favorite season, for spring had long since been
    mine.

HOW MEN DRIVE

i.

Rob ran a solid red, first car in pilgrimage
to Rocky Horror Picture show. He flicked a gaze
    back.
I didn't lose the girls? Oh, man. I think I'm in love.

You remind me of that Zeppelin line, A. said.
When you look in the mirror, baby,
baby, baby, do you like it?

All the chicks here are after Mike, Rob said.
He was wearing my feather boa.
Patted my shoulder, focus on the high heel parade.
Don't worry, don't worry.

I seen you here before, J. said.
Eyes slant under sun.
I like those jeans you got on.
I haven't seen you for awhile, the train conductor
    said.
Punched bullet holes in my ticket.
You look good, how you been?

ii.

M. said a lot but I remember nearly nothing
because I was looking at his arms
on the wheel, bone and muscle shift and pop
on sharp turns. He drove me
to the high school at night.
This was my space, he said.
The guy across had a Mustang too,
but his didn't stall.

Don't tell them it's your first show, he said.
Hand on my back now.
I took a too-deep breath. My garter belt split.
He said, They'll lipstick your forehead
and make you grind with a blow-up doll.

The poem you wrote made me cry, he said,
so I was no longer afraid of his trunk full
of rope, tarps, handsaws.
I'm still building, he said.
I'll keep cutting until I get it right.

iii.

You call me if it don't work out, J. said.
We rolled through a stop sign.
You rolled through that stop sign, the cop said
Didn't you see it?
Sorry I don't drive so careful, J. said.
Long hair spilled out a cracked window.
Now he didn't look at me.

You know how men drive? Rob said once
Red lights are stop signs,
stop signs are yield signs,
and yield signs don't exist.

CITY BOY

Sometimes I hate everything about this city,
he told me. Taxis run you over
to make a light. The garbage-river
smell in your nose. Guys that want
to make you nervous, or worse.

But there is so much more for me
& for you, who stayed behind
in a fourth floor walkup—sticky floors,
bongs & Doritos & poetry.
With you I jangled tokens,
watched the lights obscure the stars.

We saw men on corners sell blouses,
strangers light cigarettes tip to tip.
We sat on old bedspreads in the park
the rich keep pretty, watched old men
with trumpets, dogs and babies & hipsters.
We sipped forties from paper bags, because
one day we would be forty,
& Broad Street farther than a subway
where you would jump
between cars, holding my hand.

I threw my tokens into that filthy river,
full of newspapers, dead bodies
broken needles & scraps of us,
but this poem,
it wouldn't sink.

MOTHER OF THE BRIDE

One month prior
the shower of gifts begins:

red spoon rest, pink doormat,
little birds to shake salt and pepper
on meals cooked in a crock pot.

Gifts guaranteed break-resistant,
timeless, 25-year warranty.
Wine glasses. Cake knife. Lazy Susan.

Casserole dishes & candles.
Fourteen knives spearing wood.
Mostly, there are towels:

pink & blue & white, cotton,
maximum durability. Now she thinks
of her own linen closet,

the brown paisley towels
wedged in back. Planned
for slim, tan waists, but banished

to a crawlspace when the marriage
didn't happen.
Then pulled from boxes, a decade gone,

used on different bodies, long legs, wet hair,
slippery babies. The first baby
sometimes still dries her hair

with these towels, her own too new to touch.
Her mother knows the feeling well:
gift as sacred, object as altar,

love nothing short of holy.

SATURDAY AFTER CHRISTMAS, 1 AM

I-95 north home—river on my right
headlights on empty miles,
billboards cranked high.
Even trashcan fires dead now.

A detour unneeded—your house
unlit, car curbed.
With half a tank left, I
can do anything.

Do you remember spring?
Parking lot talks, firebird hair
& now something
like regret

GROCERY-DRINKS-CIGARETTES-BEAUTY

Stuck in traffic on Broad Street,
minutes shrink fast. Erie Avenue—
my great-grandfather laid tile, sailed home,
laid tile, sailed home. Stayed home.
Surely I can drive 20 blocks in 10 minutes

but I'm stopped even though *No stopping*
any time, no catcalling any time
If catcalls could carry me past rush hour,
I would ride the swell of "baby" and "princess"
like a parade float, wave at tiny sidewalk
figures from my crepe paper palace.

Southbound trains to Pattison rumble below
A token is how much? I should run underground,
maroon my car, an unlit buoy
in this sea of engines. I should count
fried chicken stands like sheep,
open my eyes & be at work.

24 hour carwash $3.74
they are always nightclub busy
& no passenger ever lets me find out why,
why do I live so far away, why do I turn off
my alarm in sleep. Cumberland, 2 minutes,
York, Dauphin, orange cones,
orange cones everywhere—

Susquehanna, 1 minute over
I am reading breathless signs
Lee's Chinese & American Food Snacks
unmoving *Natural Hair Braids Locs*
Hot Oil Quick Weaves people pack corners,
buses huff by, please, please,
let us all get where we're going

WHEN WE KNEW

It wasn't like lightning, exactly—
more like an hourglass tipped,
sands that fell like a clue,
flooded like a promise.

You told me it happened for you
in May, months after we wished
on stars like specks of amber,
or bright pennies pitched above us.

In January, I saw snowflakes
melt through dark lengths of hair.
Boots crunched ice. Colorless sky.
Fingers numb, I traced your lifeline.
I saw everything.

July, fireworks stained the sky
somewhere beyond us, sunburnt
and sand-filmy in a photo-booth.
And as October chills the air again,

I find warmth in your shoulder,
can hear you tell me in the way your hands
spread like a blanket beneath my coat,
in the way your breath catches against my neck.

A SUPERMARKET IN PENNSYLVANIA

I saw my old psychiatrist at Trader Joe's,
sampling organic hand lotion.
We last faced off

50 milligrams ago, when he talked
about stress, and I watched the clock's hands
march, an army of gears ticking

like the rattle of pills. This 2-pill-day,
I gather dried fruit, herbs,
everything organic. My old shrink,

smaller and greyer, bags peppers
and free-range chicken
with his dark-haired wife.

Tense despite the lavender plant I hold,
my gaze flings to my partner
in everything, weighing cranberries

versus apricots. He has seen me
through deflated 1-pill-days.
My old shrink has brown bags

happier than dopamine, and I want
to block his exit, show him my fruit bars
and partner, the engineer, whose perfect serotonin

levels mock health insurance. I am 8 years,
200 milligrams better. I buy only organic and
my lavender plant doesn't talk back.

I see my shrink slip away, an expired prescription.
We pay for the plant and dried cranberries,
which I have told the engineer taste best.

STITCHES

Your index fingerprint
has lifted, the reveal of a mask.

Strung up with black wire,
butterfly antennae woven

into the lace of your fingertip.
Or maybe they're a row of eyelashes,

curled and batting.
Your fingernail split

like a flat tombstone
from lightning, the mending skin

a bruised beet purple,
elsewhere, red, as if your blood

can't make up its mind.
In time the line

will pale to a faint trickle
of scar, a finger equator

where everything is warm.

ACKNOWLEDGEMENTS

Thank you to the editors of the following publications who first published many of these poems, some in slightly different form:

Aries: "After the Fire," "Mother of the Bride" (as "Bridal Shower"), "City Boy"
The Best of Philadelphia Stories: 10th Anniversary Edition: "A Supermarket in Pennsylvania"
Hawai'i Review: "Breakdown"
Philadelphia Stories: "A Supermarket in Pennsylvania," "How Men Drive" (as "Yield Signs Don't Exist")
Schuylkill Valley Journal: "Catholic Girlhood"
U.S. 1 Worksheets: "She Doesn't Know Where She Is"
Wisconsin Review: "Viewing"

Thank you also to:
Everyone at P.S. Books, especially Courtney Bambrick and Ayesha Hamid, for their incisive editing, empathy, and humor; and Carla Spataro, for creating a wonderful poetry community in Philadelphia and beyond.

Jeffrey Ethan Lee, for selecting my poem for the Sandy Crimmins Prize.

Marie Kane, invaluable teacher and friend, for her encouragement and guidance.

Allison Mosher, for creating the stunningly beautiful cover art.

Chris Pomrink, for being so quotable.

Cecilia Morgnanesi, Pat Ionata, Kristin Ionata, Michael Ryan, Kathryn Morgnanesi, Orlando Morgnanesi, Elisa Ionata, and Vincenzo Ionata, whose love and support mean the world to me.